Walruses
For Kids

Amazing Animal Books for Young Readers

By Kim Chase

Mendon Cottage Books

JD-Biz Publishing

Download Free Books!
http://MendonCottageBooks.com

Read More Amazing Animal Books

Purchase at Amazon.com

Download Free Books!
http://MendonCottageBooks.com

Table of Contents

Introduction

Welcome to the wonderful world of walruses! Have you ever wondered about those amazing sea creatures? Did you ever want to know why they have such long tusks, or why they have so many whiskers?

There are so many interesting things to learn about the walruses. Find the answers to questions such as where do they live, and what do they eat? Come along as we explore more about those noisy mammals that live in the freezing cold icy waters in the North.

Information On Walruses

Walruses are easy to spot. They have many interesting features. Their long white ivory tusks are what people usually notice first. These tusks are actually long canine teeth. The walruses use their tusks to help them do many things. They use their tusks to grip onto the ice or land. Then they use these strong tusks to haul their large bodies out of the icy water they live in. Other times, they use these tusks to make holes in the ice. These holes are known as "breathing holes". These breathing holes allow the walruses to come up for air when they are searching for food in the water below. The walruses also use their tusks to protect themselves from danger.

Some of the other features you may have noticed about the walrus are their thick rows of whiskers (known as mystacial vibrissae), their blubbery looking bodies and their flippers. Each one of these features plays an important role. Their mystacial vibrissae (whiskers) are very sensitive, and helps the walrus find food that may be hiding near the ocean's dark floor. Their whiskers are very sensitive to touch. The blubber on the walruses' body helps them to keep warm in the icy cold region they call home. Another interesting thing about the walruses are their flippers. Walruses have both back and front flippers. Their front flippers are webbed, and look like they have five fingers (digits.) Their back flipper looks like the shape of a triangle. When walruses are on land, they can actually turn their back flippers so that they can walk on all four!

Walruses are known as mammals. They spend a great deal of time in the water, but walruses also spend time on land as well. You can find walruses resting on pack ice, ice floes (floating ice) or sunning themselves along the beaches by the water's edge. Although the walruses may look bald, they do actually have fur. Their fur is a brownish red, almost cinnamon in color. The scientific name for a walrus is Odobenus rosmarus.

Walruses are very big, and can also be very noisy. Depending on which type of walrus they are, their size can vary from over 7 ft. to as big as 14 ft. long. Walruses can weigh as much as 3,700 lbs!

The walruses can be divided up into two groups based on where they live. These two groups are known as the Atlantic Walrus, and the Pacific Walrus. The Atlantic Walrus is usually smaller in size than the Pacific Walrus. The Pacific Walruses are the biggest of all the walruses, and their tusks are also the longest. There are also more Pacific Walruses than there are Atlantic Walruses.

Facts About Walruses

Walruses are very social creatures that like to gather in herds. The size of their herds can range in number anywhere from 100 walruses to more than 1,000! An adult male walrus is called a bull. The female walrus is called a cow.

The reason that walruses lay in the sun is to keep warm. Although their color is usually a reddish brown, when they lay in the sun, their skin can turn pink in color. It is actually good when their skin color changes to pink. That is a sign that the walrus is warming up. The walrus also has its thick blubber to protect them and keep them warm from the freezing cold waters of the Artic. This layer of blubber is under the skin of the walrus, and can measure to over 5" thick.

When walruses are young, their coat is a deep colored brown. As the walruses grow older, this color begins to change. Their color gets lighter, and looks more reddish brown. When male walruses become old, the color of their skin turns mostly pink. When a walrus is swimming, they can look almost white in color. This is because the cold water makes their skin blood vessels become tighter and narrower.

A walrus can stay up to 30 minutes underwater before they must surface for air. The walrus can actually slow down their heartbeat so that they can stand up to the icy cold Artic water temperatures. Most groups of walrus will travel south for the winter months, then turn around and head north for the summer.

The male walruses have air sacs that can be found by their neck. These air sacs are very useful. One thing it helps them to do is make loud, deep roaring sounds. These sacs can also fill up with air. When they inflate, the walrus can stay afloat in the water vertically so that he can go to sleep. Their nostrils stay closed when they are resting.

Both the female and the male walruses have tusks, but it is the males' tusks that are slightly longer. These tusks will continue to grow over their lifetime. A female's tusk can measure 2-½ ft long, while, a male's tusk can measure over 3 ft. long! The scientific name for walrus is Odobenus rosmarus. In Latin, this name actually means, "tooth walking sea horse".

The walruses' whiskers, also known as mystacial vibrissae, are also very interesting. They can have as many as 13 to 15 rows of whiskers that are 12" long. That could mean as many as 400 to 700 total whiskers! Many times, walruses that live in the wild, do not have whiskers that reach that long. They are always using their whiskers to look for food at the ocean's bottom, so their whiskers are shorter.

The walruses' eyesight is not very good, but they do have excellent hearing as well as an excellent sense of smell. An Eskimo imitated the sounds of a walrus, and another walrus from as far away as one mile answered back! Walruses like to be near each other. Touch is another important sense for the walrus. The average life span for a walrus living in the wild is from 20 – 40 years.

Pacific Walruses

Most of the Walruses are Pacific Walruses. The estimated number of Pacific Walruses is more than 200,000. A male walrus can weigh between 1,800 up to 3,700 lbs. One of the largest reported males weighed in at an amazing 4,400 lbs.! This is very unusual, because they do not usually get that big. The females usually weight about 1,750 lbs. These walruses can measure between 7 to 12 feet long. The Pacific Walrus is darker in color and bigger in size than the Atlantic Walruses.

The Pacific Walruses can be found living in the seas to the North of Alaska and Russia. They can be spotted in the Laptev, Chukchi, and Bering Sea. The Laptev Sea is just South of the Artic Ocean, near

Siberia in the northern part of Russia. The Chukchi Sea is in the southern part of the Artic Ocean off of the Alaskan northwest coast. The Bering Sea is South of the Chukchi Sea. The Bearing Sea is the furthest South the Walruses travel.

The walruses travel south in the winter. They can be seen on pack ice in the Bering Sea, or in waters near Siberia in Russia. The walruses travel North in the summer, and enjoy the waters of the Chukchi Sea in northern Alaska.

Arctic Walruses

The Atlantic Walruses live in a coastal region that stretches from the northeastern part of Canada, and over to Greenland in what is considered to be the Canadian Arctic. These Atlantic Walruses weight less than the Pacific Walruses do. The Atlantic male walruses weigh in at about 2,000 lbs. The average female weighs in at about 1,200 lbs, but there are some smaller females that weigh only 880 lbs. The Atlantic Walrus is usually lighter in color than the Pacific Walruses are, and have a more flattened snout, and shorter tusks.

Baby Walruses

A baby walrus is also called a calf. They can weigh anywhere between 75 to 165 lbs. when they are born. The calves vary in length from 3.5 to 4.5 feet. Many of the Pacific Walruses are born during their migration. Most of the calves are born in the months between April through June. The newborn walruses are able to swim from the time they are born.

Newborn calves are born with a gray coat and only a small layer of blubber to keep them warm. Their coats turn from this grayish color to a more reddish brown color, as they get older.

The calves usually stay with their mothers for up to two years. It is not uncommon to see newborn and baby walruses being carried around on their mother's back. The reason for this is that the mother's are trying to keep the babies safe from harm. If a herd of walruses that are resting on land get startled, this will cause the male walruses to stampede to the water for safety. Because they are in such a rush, the calves can get crushed. So if the mother carries the baby on her back, she can try to get them to a safer place, and avoid them from being crushed. Other times the mother walrus will also hold the calf between her flippers, to keep them protected.

The mother walruses try to stay close to their babies, but they must search for food. This is a dangerous time for the baby calves, because they are left all alone and unprotected on the ice.

How Walruses Communicate

Walruses like to gather together with other walruses. When they are grouped together in a large number on the ice packs, ice floes, or on the rocky beaches, they are known as a herd.

The skin of the walrus is not sensitive to touch. But their whiskers are very sensitive. One of the ways walruses speak to each other is by touching whiskers. Each whisker has a nerve ending of its own. So when the walruses touch each other by the whiskers, this sends a positive feeling to their brain.

Walruses are also known to be very loud. They communicate with each other by using their vocal cords. These vocal cords make it possible for them to make noises both in the water and on land. The male walruses have air sacs in their neck. Because of these air sacs, the males can make sounds from under the water that sound like bells. These bell like sounds are used to warn other walruses about dangers like predators that may be near. They also use this sound to call and find other walruses when they are in the water.

The walruses make many different sounds like clicking, grunting, barking and whistling. Sometimes a young calf will bellow loudly if they feel like they are in danger.

The mother walruses try and teach their young to make sounds. The young calves quickly learn the sounds that their mothers make, and the mothers learn the sounds their young calves make. This type of communication is very important especially if the baby calf ever gets separated from their mother. The mother can quickly find her young.

Male walruses can be very aggressive. Often times, the bigger the walrus the more aggressive they are. Aggression is one way that they use to see who will be in charge. When a walrus becomes aggressive, they can be seen trying to scare the walruses that are around them. They scare the other walruses by coughing, roaring or sometimes even snorting.

Walruses' Habitat

Walruses can be found living in the icy cold shallow waters close to the Artic Circle. The waters in these places are usually less than 262 feet deep. They also spend time a great deal of time on land. The walruses like to lie out on pack ice or ice floes. Ice is their first choice, but if they cannot find ice, then they will lay on the water's edge on rocky small islands. When the walruses are on land sunning themselves, you will find them huddled together in large numbers. This large group of walruses is called a herd.

Walruses' Diet

Clams are the favorite food for walruses. In fact, in one meal they can eat up to as many as 4,000 clams! Walruses also enjoy eating mussels, oysters, scallops, snails, fish, sea cucumbers, urchins and starfish.

One of the ways that the walruses find their food is to spray water from their mouth and aim it at the sea bottom. By squirting this water, it moves the mud around so that they can find any food that may have been hiding there. Once the food is no longer hidden, the walruses can then feel the food with their whiskers.

It is interesting how the walruses eat the meat of the clam. They actually vacuum out the meat! This is done when they seal their strong lips to the clam and quickly move their tongue up and down inside their mouth. When they do this, it forms a tight seal, and that is how they suction out the meat!

Where Do Walruses Come From?

Have you ever wondered where these mustached, long toothed walruses of today ever evolved from? There is still much to learn, and at this point, their evolution process is still not totally clear. But from DNA found on early fossils, it is believed that they are actually related to an earlier form of the bear family. A walrus is also a close match to a seal. The biggest difference between the walrus and the seal is that the seals don't grow tusks. The Saber Toothed Cat is another close relation to the walrus. The reason for this is because their jaws are very much alike.

Some experts think that there used to be more species of walruses, but they were not able to change enough to survive. It is believed that a species of walrus existed in the warm tropics region. Walruses looked for the colder areas for them to survive.

For the walrus, the biggest part of their evolution was when their appendages changed over to flippers. They could easily get around in the water thanks to their flippers, and their large size did not matter. The walruses' back flipper can grasp onto things, and has what looks like five fingers.

It is thought that the reason why the walrus went to live in the water instead of on land is because it was too hot for them on land. They needed the colder waters so they could cool their bodies down. Once the Ice Age started, the walrus was able to change so that they could live in the coldest regions.

It is amazing that the walruses were able to adapt to their surroundings and live for over a million years. The walruses are very smart and strong. Even today, these large animals are adapting and still evolving. Global warming has caused their waters to become warmer, and they need to adapt in order to live.

The walruses' future does look bright because of the efforts of many to stop the global warming problem. Right now, there are enough walruses to make sure that they will be here for many centuries to come.

Seals and Walruses

The walrus and the seal are alike in many ways. They share some of the same features such as the shape of their bodies, and how they swim. Just like the seals, when a walrus swims, they move their whole body and do not use their flippers as much. Another thing they have in common is that they can also move their rear flippers to face forward, so that they can move around on all four flippers. Both the walrus and the seal do not have any external ears.

The walrus is part of the pinniped species. A pinniped is a Latin word meaning "fin footed". Seals and Walruses are both part of the pinniped group. These Pinnipeds have a thick layer of blubber that insulates them and helps to keep them warm in the icy water. Based on their weight, these Pinnipeds have more blood than many other mammals. This helps them to have enough oxygen for their long dives underwater while they are searching for food.

Life in the Herd

One of the things that the walruses do decide on is who will be in charge of their herd. There are a few things that the walruses use to decide this. This system of who is in charge of the herd is referred to as the social structure or hierarchy. So how are these walruses chosen? Some factors have to do with size, such as the size of the walrus, their tusk size, and how aggressive they are. Many times, those walruses chosen to be in charge of the herd will be challenged to hold onto their title. Other walruses that hold a lower level position in their social structure will challenge them.

Walruses are very social animals and enjoy gathering in large herds. Over a course of a lifetime, the herd that a walrus belongs to can change. The male and the female walrus will form different herds. The male herds will form their own male herd, while the females will form a herd of their own. The baby calves will stay with their mothers in the female herd. The mothers and calves usually stay together for about two years.

One way of knowing how old a walrus is by the length of their tusks. These tusks will usually stop growing when the walrus reaches the age of 15. If the walrus should break their tusk, this will cause them to fall down in their social standing in the herd.

Walrus Features

There are many features that come to mind when you think of a walrus. Probably the first feature you may think of is their large, long ivory tusks. Both the male and the female walruses have tusks. However, the male tusks are thicker and longer than the females.

There are many other features to this amazing sea creature. They have faces that are small, but do not have any external ears. Their face has row upon row of large whiskers. The walruses also have a thick neck area. Their bodies have many layers of blubbery fat that help them to keep warm. This becomes important since they live in freezing conditions near the Artic.

The males generally weigh more than the female walruses do. The Pacific Walruses tend to weigh more than the Atlantic Walruses. The male walrus can weigh near 4,400 pounds, while the females can weigh nearly 3,000 pounds. Their body has a round shape.

Their rear flippers are shaped like a triangle, with five digits made of bone. These back flippers are also bumpy to help the walrus hold onto the ice as they move along. The flippers have a very thick skin that adapts well to both water and land. These flippers stay close to their bodies when they swim and help them to steer. On land, they can push their front flippers outward to help them walk on them.

Walruses and Humans

Walruses and humans have come in contact with each other for a long time. Unfortunately this relationship has not always been a good one for the walrus. From early on, humans have hunted the walrus and nearly drove them to extinction more than once. People living in the regions of the Artic relied on the walrus for many things. They hunted the walrus to help them survive, and were used as food. They were also hunted for their ivory tusks, and the hunters also created tools that helped them to live in such a harsh place like the Artic.

Even today, the walruses are still being hunted. The difference is that now there are a set number of walruses that can be killed. The only people allowed to hunt walruses are the people that are native to the Artic region. Sadly, there are reports that poachers (people that hunt when they are not allowed to) are still out there hunting walruses.

Before it was banned, hundreds of walruses were hunted because of their beautiful ivory tusks. Thankfully, there are now other ways to make ivory that work just as well and costs less. Because of this, the demand for ivory isn't as great as it once was.

Even though walruses are very strong and fierce fighters, humans are usually safe from them. The walrus does not attack a human without a reason. Walruses will do whatever they can to protect their young as well as themselves. There have been reports of hunters who have gotten hurt or who have even died because they were not prepared for how aggressive a walrus can be, or from their shear strength.

Walruses seem sensitive to noise. This can cause a big problem for them especially when the walruses are on land. When the loud roar of an airplane's engine flies over them, it causes the walrus to become startled and scared. The first thing they want to do is head for the water where they will feel it will be safer for them. This is not as easy as it sounds. When there are hundreds of walruses trying to do this all the same time, it causes a stampede. It is during this stampede that the some of the older and younger walruses get trampled. To try and stop this from happening, there have been efforts made to stop air flights from flying over the areas where the walruses are known to live.

Migration

When an animal moves from one place to another, this is known as migration. When the walruses migrate, they appear to follow the pack ice. There is not much known about the Atlantic Walruses, but it seems that they do not move around very much, and stay in the same general area all year round.

The Pacific Walruses on the other hand, have been known to travel over 1,800 miles each year! Both the Pacific female walruses, as well as their young, seem to travel more than the male Pacific Walruses do. These walruses spend their winters in the south and central areas of the

Bering Sea. During the summer months, the Pacific Walruses head north to the Chukchi Sea.

Swimming is the usual way that the Pacific Walruses use to migrate. Sometimes, they may catch a ride on a passing ice floe. The baby walruses are born during their migration north toward the Chukchi Sea. During this time, thousands of male walruses stay behind in the southern part of the Bering Sea. Then, as the ice starts to melt, these males head for land, and will haul out on the rocky islands. Ooglit is the Eskimo name given for when walruses are gathered together on land in their haul out.

Living in Cold Water

When you think about it, isn't it amazing how the walruses can live in such icy cold water? There are many things that a walrus can do to help them cope and adapt to these frigid temperatures.

The walruses' average speed for swimming is just over 4 mph. They can have a quick burst, and swim as fast as 21 mph! But this can only be done for a short time. Walruses need to breathe for one minute at the water's surface. This breathing needs to be done for each time they have spent up to eight minutes underwater.

The walrus can breathe both through their mouth, as well as through their nose! When a walrus is underwater, there is a muscle that will block any water from going down their throat as they open their mouth to breathe.

It is also interesting how a walrus's body heat helps them to deal with living in such a cold place. A walrus will lose more of their body's heat quicker in the water than they do in the air. This heat loss can be 27 times quicker!

The average body temperature of a walrus is just under 98 F. A walrus can keep their skin temperature warmer than the surrounding water they are in. This temperature range can be anywhere from 1.8 to 5.4 F. Walruses have been found in water as cold as –31 F!

It comes as no surprise that the walrus does have a heavy layer of fat called blubber. This blubber helps to insulate them against the cold. But what you may not have known is that in the freezing cold winter months, this fat layer can be about one third of their whole body mass!

Walruses Are Endangered

Walruses are considered an endangered species. The Atlantic Walrus used to be found in Nova Scotia, and sometimes as far to the south as Massachusetts. Commercial hunters were responsible for reducing the number of these walruses. In 1972, an act was passed to protect them. The only ones allowed to hunt these walruses are the native people of the land, and even then, they are only allowed to hunt a certain amount of walruses.

There are a great many things that threaten the walrus. Orcas (killer whales), polar bears as well as humans all hunt the walrus. Humans would kill the walruses for their oil and ivory tusks.

One of the Walruses' biggest threats is climate change. It has made a big change where they live. Walruses depend on sea ice for many things. One of the things the sea ice does is provide food for the walruses. The sea ice is an important part of their food web.

From the ends of this ice grows algae. Zooplankton is a small animal that eats the algae. The Zooplankton are then eaten by larger animals. There are nutrients and food particles that go down to the floor of the ocean. These particles and nutrients feed large beds of clams and other mollusks on the ocean's floor. The walruses then eat these clams and mollusks.

The climate change has caused the sea ice to shrink. With less sea ice, there is less food. So the mother walruses need to travel further away to find food. This leaves the walrus calves alone and helpless on the ice, and could be hunted by the orcas or polar bears.

Pictures of Walruses

Mother and Baby – Photo

Getting warm in the sun

Sense of touch is important to walruses

Walrus family hang out

About the Author

Kim Chase

Kim Chase is a published author of children's books. She lives in Ocala, Florida, and has written a book series for pre-school aged children. In addition, she has also published a short story mystery for young adults. Kim loves to write, and enjoys spending time outdoors with her two beautiful horses.

Top Ten Dog Breeds For Kids
Amazing Animal Books For Young Readers
Kisha Bennett & John Davidson

German Shepherds
Dog Books for Kids
K. Bennett

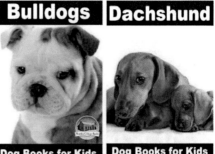

Bulldogs
Dog Books for Kids
K. Bennett

Dachshund
Dog Books for Kids
K. Bennett

Poodles
Dog Books for Kids
K. Bennett

Labrador Retrievers
Dog Books for Kids
K. Bennett

Rottweilers
Dog Books for Kids
K. Bennett

Boxers
Dog Books for Kids
K. Bennett

Golden Retrievers
Dog Books for Kids
K. Bennett

Puppies
Dog Books For Kids
Amazing Animal Books
By John Davidson

Beagles
Dog Books for Kids
K. Bennett

Yorkshire Terriers
Dog Books for Kids
K. Bennett

Dogs
Top Ten Dog Breeds For Kids
Amazing Animal Books For Young Readers
Zahra Jazeel & John Davidson

Cats For Kids
Amazing Animal Books For Young Readers
K. Bennett & John Davidson

Foxes For Kids
Amazing Animal Books For Young Readers
Zahra Jazeel & John Davidson

Wolves For Kids
Amazing Animal Books For Young Readers
By John Davidson and Virginia Fidler

Our books are available at

1. Amazon.com
2. Barnes and Noble
3. Itunes
4. Kobo
5. Smashwords
6. Google Play Books

Download Free Books!
http://MendonCottageBooks.com

Publisher

JD-Biz Corp

P O Box 374

Mendon, Utah 84325

http://www.jd-biz.com/

Mendon Cottage Books

P O Box 374, Mendon Utah 84325